C0-AWE-315

FACING THE MUSIC

PAUL AUSTER

Station Hill

PS
3551
.U77
F3

Grateful acknowledgement to *Ironwood* and *Pequod* in
which some of these poems first appeared.

Published by Station Hill Press in Barrytown & produced
at Open Studio in Rhinebeck, New York, with generous
assistance from the New York State Council on the Arts &
the National Endowment for the Arts.

Copyright © 1980 by Paul Auster
All rights reserved

ISBN 0-930794-29-x

Credo

The infinite

tiny things. For once merely to breathe
in the light of the infinite

tiny things
that surround us. Or nothing
can escape

the lure of this darkness, the eye
will discover that we are
only what has made us less
than we are. To say nothing. To say:
our very lives

depend on it.

ST. OLAF COLLEGE LIBRARY

Obituary in the Present Tense

It is all one to him—
where he begins

and where he ends. Egg white, the white
of his eye: he says
bird milk, sperm

sliding from the word
of himself. For the eye
is evanescent,
clings only to what is, no more here

or less there, but everywhere, every

thing. He memorizes
none of it. Nor does he write

anything down. He abstains
from the heart

of living things. He waits.

And if he begins, he will end,
as if his eye had opened in the mouth

of a bird, as if he had never begun

to be anywhere. He speaks

from distances
no less far than these.

Narrative

Because what happens will never happen,
and because what has happened
endlessly happens again,

we are as we were, everything
has changed in us, if we speak
of the world
it is only to leave the world

unsaid. Early winter: the yellow apples still
unfallen
in a naked tree, the tracks
of invisible deer

in the first snow, and then the snow
that does not stop. We repent
of nothing. As if we could stand
in this light. As if we could stand in the silence
of this single moment

of light.

S.A. 1911-1979

From loss. And from such loss
that marauds the mind—even to the loss

of mind. To begin with this thought: without rhyme

or reason. And then simply to wait. As if the first word
comes only after the last, after a life
of waiting for the word

that was lost. To say no more
than the truth of it: men die, the world fails, the words

have no meaning. And therefore to ask
only for words.

Stone wall. Stone heart. Flesh and blood.

As much as all this.
More.

Search for a Definition

(On Seeing a Painting by Bradley Walker Tomlin)

Always the smallest act

possible
in this time of acts

larger than life, a gesture
toward the thing that passes

almost unseen. A small wind

disturbing a bonfire, for example,
which I found the other day
by accident

on a museum wall. Almost nothing
is there: a few wisps
of white

thrown idly against the pure black
background, no more
than a small gesture
trying to be nothing

more than itself. And yet
it is not here
and to my eyes will never become
a question
of trying to simplify
the world, but a way of looking for a place

to enter the world, a way of being
present
among the things
that do not want us—but which we need
to the same measure that we need
ourselves. Only a moment before
the beautiful

woman
who stood beside me
had been saying how much she wanted
a child
and how time was beginning
to run out on her. We said
we must each write a poem
using the words 'a small
wind

disturbing a bonfire.' Since that time
nothing

has meant more than the small
act
present in these words, the act
of trying to speak

words

that mean almost nothing. To the very end
I want to be equal

to whatever it is
my eye will bring me, as if
I might finally see myself

let go
in the nearly invisible
things

that carry us along with ourselves and all
the unborn children

into the world.

Between the Lines

Stone-pillowed, the ways
of remoteness. And written in your palm,
the road.

Home, then, is not home
but the distance between
blessed
and unblessed. And whoever puts himself
into the skin
of his brother, will know
what sorrow is
to the seventh year
beyond the seventh year
of the seventh year.

And divide his children in half.

And wrestle in darkness
with an angel.

In Memory of Myself

Simply to have stopped.

As if I could begin
where my voice has stopped, myself
the sound of a word

I cannot speak.

So much silence
to be brought to life
in this pensive flesh, the beating
drum of words
within, so many words

lost in the wide world
within me, and thereby to have known
that in spite of myself

I am here.

As if this were the world.

ST OLAF COLLEGE LIBRARY

Bedrock

Dawn as an image
of dawn, and the very sky collapsing
into itself. Irreducible

image
of pure water, the pores of earth
exuding light: such yield

as only light will bring, and the very stones
undead

in the image of themselves.

The consolation of color.

Facing the Music

Blue. And within that blue a feeling
of green, the gray blocks of clouds
buttressed against air, as if
in the idea of rain
the eye
could master the speech
of any given moment

on earth. Call it the sky. And so
to describe
whatever it is
we see, as if it were nothing
but the idea
of something we had lost
within. For we can begin
to remember

the hard earth, the flint
reflecting stars, the undulating
oaks set loose
by the heaving of air, and so down
to the least seed, revealing what grows
above us, as if
because of this blue there could be
this green

that spreads, myriad
and miraculous
in this, the most silent

moment of summer. Seeds
speak of this juncture, define
where the air and the earth erupt
in this profusion of chance, the random
forces of our own lack
of knowing what it is
we see, and merely to speak of it
is to see
how words fail us, how nothing comes right
in the saying of it, not even these words
I am moved to speak
in the name of this blue
and green
that vanish into the air
of summer.

             Impossible
to hear it anymore. The tongue
is forever taking us away
from where we are, and nowhere
can we be at rest
in the things we are given
to see, for each word
is an elsewhere, a thing that moves
more quickly than the eye, even
as this sparrow moves, veering
into the air
in which it has no home. I believe, then,
in nothing

these words might give you, and still
I can feel them
speaking through me, as if
this alone

is what I desire, this blue
and this green, and to say
how this blue
has become for me the essence
of this green, and more than the pure
seeing of it, I want you to feel
this word
that has lived inside me
all day long, this
desire for nothing

but the day itself, and how it has grown
inside my eyes, stronger
than the word it is made of, as if
there could never be another word

that would hold me
without breaking.

(1978-1979)

*This book was produced in April 1980
at the Open Studio Print Shop in Rhinebeck, New York
in an edition limited to 1000 copies
43 of which are signed and numbered by the author.*

PS 3551 .U77 F3

Auster, Paul, 1947-

Facing the music

DEMCO